Words to Color By

25 Inspirational Coloring Pages

JENNIFER LANKENAU

DIVERSIONBOOKS

Diversion Books
A Division of Diversion Publishing Corp.
443 Park Avenue South, Suite 1008
New York, New York 10016
www.DiversionBooks.com

For more information, email info@diversionbooks.com

First Diversion Books edition August 2016.
Print ISBN: 978-1-68230-227-9

BE BRAVE

GREAT THINGS

TAKE TIME

NURTURE

YOUR WEIRD

TIME IS

THE KEY

Life is in the Details

STRENGTH IS

Beautiful

The end is just

A new beginning.

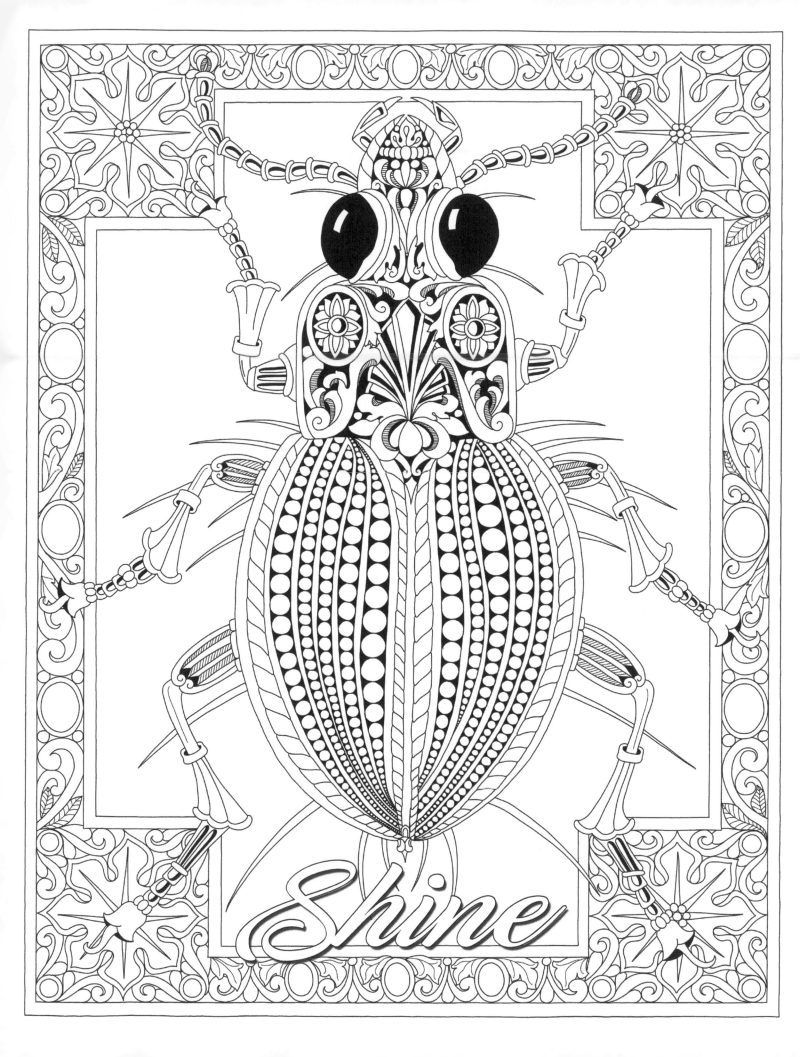

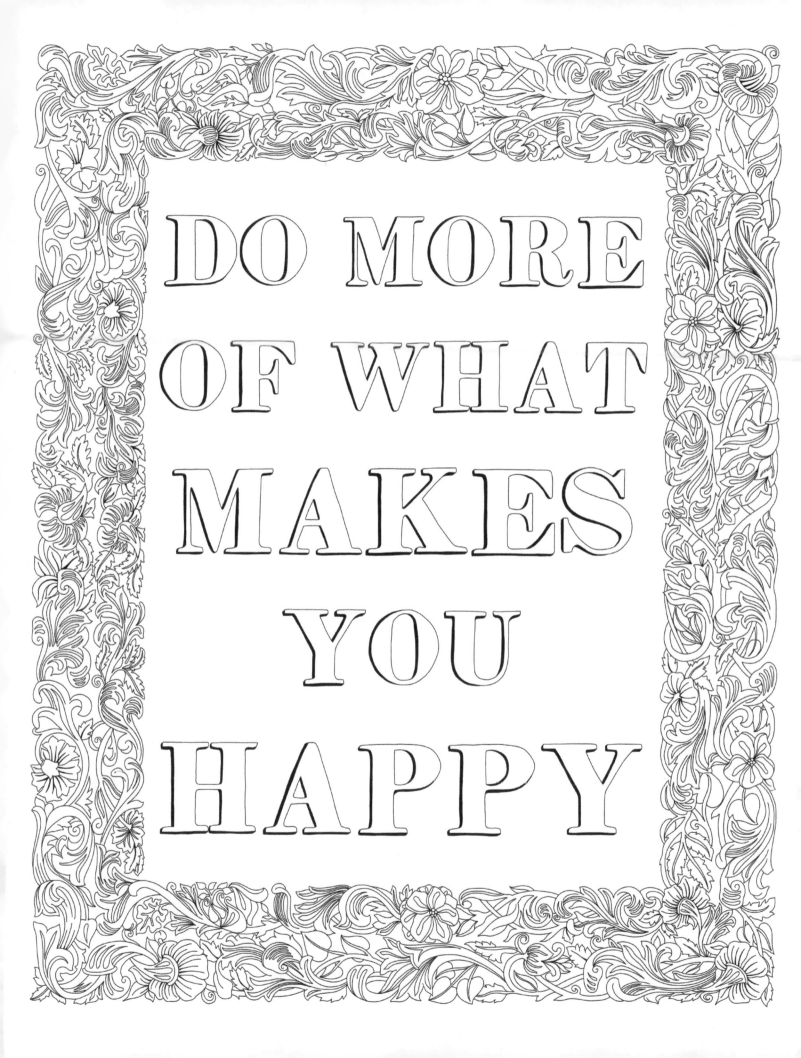

Printed in the USA
CPSIA information can be obtained
at www.ICGtesting.com
JSHW072027140824
68134JS00042B/3814